I0698423

Blank Book

Copyright © 2014

Speedy Publishing LLC
40 E. Main St., #1156,
Newark, DE 19711
www.speedypublishing.co

Publisher's Note: This is a work of fiction. Names, characters, places, and incidents are a product of the author's imagination. Locales and public names are sometimes used for atmospheric purposes. Any resemblance to actual people, living or dead, or to businesses, companies, events, institutions, or locales is completely coincidental.

Speedy Publishing LLC©2014

Ordering Information:
Quantity sales. Special discounts are available on quantity purchases by corporations, associations, and others. For details, contact the "Special Sales Department" at the address above.

Blank Book -- 1st ed.
ISBN 978-1-6328795-3-0